Black Dog Dreaming

Michael Dubhthaigh

ISBN-13: **978-1973790990**

ISBN-10: 1973790998

DEDICATION

To the poor bastards who were unfortunate enough to come into contact with me over the past 40 odd years.

Acknowledgments

To Shelley, who told me the word Stressed is Desserts spelt backwards. My landlady, who tolerates my tardiness.

CONTENTS

CHAPTER 1.

Hard at work and last job of the day, fitting a frameless glass door into the hinges of a wall anchored glass panel. Finish this, clean up, get paid and out of there, job done.

A slight slip and the bottom corner of the glass door hits the tiles. The door shatters, showering me with glass, I quickly drop my head downwards to avoid the shattering glass coming down on me, I see blood pouring out of an artery down my hands that were still gripping shattered glass and onto tiles and about 30kg of glass scattered across the bath room floor.

I felt the warmth of blood flowing down my neck and chest. I got out of there, out into the yard, and the lady of the house got me some compression bandages and we waited for an Ambulance.

Sitting on the grass, trying to stem the flow of blood from my cuts, I looked back in through the door way and thought a good job turned to crap at the last minute. The story of my life.

The night before this accident I had spent about 3 hours setting up an ad to post on face book. A good clear photo, check the links were working, the add to cart. Audience selection, digging through face books audience feature, so many choices, follow the procedure, can't have it to big or to small, just a test.

But like the frame less door, ad test number 23 turned to crap too, although not as shattering an experience as the door. It ended with a quiet whimper, I think it reached an audience of 787 with 12 website views and no sales.

Sitting there on the grass I looked at the blood leaking from numerous cuts and thought how painless and peaceful it would be to bleed to death.

Michael Dubhthaigh

I was amazed at how quickly the blood flowed from the cuts in my veins, probably the last couple of minutes might be the most stressful as the heart and other organs shut down due to a lack of blood.

After the nurses at the hospital had finished with me and told me not to do much of anything for at least a week, then go and see my doctor to have the stitches removed.

I spent the week looking back, because up to this point it had been one disaster after another. Actually my whole life had been a roller coaster of very few highs and lots of lows and lowers. I thought a lot in that week.

Michael Dubhthaigh

CHAPTER 2

I kept bees for a hobby. I think they are interesting and they make a good product. The end of 2016 had been good, I had my hives about 100klms north of where I live. Bees were a type of therapy for me.

I was driving a truck and working long hours, mostly at night. I am not married, and live on my own and every so often I would have a few days off and work my bees, chat with the property owners, extract the honey, store the wax, deliver honey to a couple of clients I had. That was the extent of my social life.

I sold most in bulk and kept some for 2 store owners near me. This broke the cycle of loneliness of being on my own, most of my driving was at night, hours spent staring at a white line, looking out for animals, talking to the moon, (if it was out), singing, I think if I had a good voice I would have been a good singer !.

But the end of 2016 was good. Compliments from many who had bought my latest batch of honey, things were looking good going into 2017.

The first week of January started off okay, back to the grindstone that was work, then it rained for 3 weeks. During the second week of wet weather I was looking for a break in the weather to visit my bees, I had not left them a lot of stores after my last rob and I knew they would struggle with hive beetle infestation if they could not get out and forage.

When the sun finally came out I took a couple of days off work and went up to the bees, I had lost two hives to hive beetle, even with a new system under the brood boxes to trap the hive beetle, but with the humid wet weather the traps should have been cleared weekly to give the bees any chance. Still, I had 7 hives left, and I was thinking I should not have sold a couple I had split late in 2016.

February into March and things at work were not going well. 3+ years of constantly working nights, sleeping through the day, or combinations of both was taking its toll. I needed a break.

Black Dog Dreaming

The wet weather was also getting to me frustrating other things I wanted to do. Sometimes I would just get my boots off and the phone would go off asking if I could do another run.

More than once I had just climbed into bed and the phone went off, timed to the very second that I was about to close my eyes. The joys of 24/7 on call work. Very different after being in building most of my working life, set hours and always people around. The body clock was out of control.

Waking about 2 pm one wet, humid March day, and wondering whether to have breakfast or lunch, but feeling something was wrong because everything seem gray, the day, my mind, I could not see color in anything, everything was in slow motion. The black dog was visiting me.

The phone rang asking me if I could be ready in an hour to load for a 13 hour round trip. I said, "No, It feels like I am in a strange place". I answered the "what on earth are you talking about" with a simple "don't know, but it feels scary".

A day or so later I rejected the offers of come around and have a chat and a few beers.

It took about 4 days to get over that bout of depression, I don't remember much except that I was in a dark, scary place. I remember lying on the lounge with the TV remote but don't remember if I turned the TV on.

A couple of weeks later I pulled the pin on that job. The pay was basic, it was time for me to move on. I had been wanting to do it for ages but that job left little opportunity to look anywhere or to get on the grapevine and find out what was going on.

So what to do? I had little in the way of savings, some debt, few friends, 3 years of living and mostly working alone did little for my social life.

My family live about 800 klms away (in both directions). My bees were only a hobby, so I set about making some more boxes, bought new frames and wax.

Making the boxes was no big deal, making the frames and laying wax in

Michael Dubhthaigh

them is a very tedious process, and to be honest I never really had my heart in it. It was more like I was doing it for something to do. For me 7 – 10 hives was enough.

I had nearly 4 years of being ruled by a phone 24/7, I wanted variety, expand my life, not move from one cocoon to another.

I was starting to enjoy this freedom of not anticipating a phone call asking me to get ready to go somewhere. My fitness was beginning to improve. My head was still screwed, thinking of the pros and cons of whether increasing my apiary was the way to go.

Bigger expenses, and lots more work, I kept thinking at my age do I really need it?, bigger vehicle, find more sites, more management. Really I wanted complete change, otherwise It is only the same track, different circuit. My resume was going out and not getting replies.

I have for years received emails promoting currency trading, shares, lifestyle, dating, all sorts of things and like everyone else, I read some, and deleted them, a couple of the more interesting I probably asked for more information, one or two I probably tried, failed and got a refund. I was in a mode for change and had the time to sit back and read these things. Beside with the rainy weather there was not much else to do.

During March I replied to one getting more information about setting up a website and drop shipping. looking at the previews I saw they were spending big on face book ads to get a return.

Looking back at all this analysis I realised my mind was still in dream mode. I was reading what I wanted to see. It fitted the narrative I wanted, at this point in time I really had nothing else going for me, and if it didn't work there was a rope and a sturdy tree in the back yard.

In my dreamy outlook I could see the cons like, you would have to keep finding new products to sell once one ran its course, but I see that often on T.V. they move from one new gadget to another, and I

guess they must do alright because they have been doing it for years.

Michael Dubhthaigh

So I thought if Keleva products could do it on T.V. week in week out and had been doing it for years under various names, then this FB program would be worth a shot, put in the time and effort, plus they offered all the tools, all the back up you needed. What could go wrong?.

It wasn't as if I was totally a novice at this. I had played with selling things on the internet in years past, back in the day when e-bay was gaining momentum, I knew about drop shipping, for about 3 years I had a site on Artfire drop shipping hand made necklaces and golf ball markers, etc. It worked well, I never made a lot, but enough to keep me interested, and it helped keep old mate in work. I did pay big bucks for an Amazon affiliate site which made bugger all.

I signed up, forking over $3,500.00 au., 60 days, and if it doesn't work I will bail out. So into the training and follow the lessons, on my way to making $100,000 a year on line. Ask a few questions, set up a store, start searching for products in my niches. Hours and hours on a computer. Try this, try that, run test ads. Nada!. Stuff this give it a break. I was just helping face book improve their bottom line.

So nearly 6 weeks with this drop shipping thing and not a razoo. Idiot I thought, sucked in by the hype. Get a real job.

I had been still flicking my resume around to different employers and not getting much response. I put an ad in a free paper looking for handy man work I needed to have some sort of cash flow,

I did a couple of quotes and a few days later one of them was accepted. I was happy to have someone give me a job doing a renovation for them, not a big job, but at least it was some cash flow, and my eyes could re adjust from looking at a screen to looking at the world, and physical activity is always good.

I was still putting some time into my bees which were coming ok. I robbed them again, but left them plenty of food this time, only taking about 40 kgs from 7 hives, to fill an order for a customer.

Not a lot of money from that. I needed to be getting serious about finding

Michael Dubhthaigh

alternative sources of income. So back to this drop ship thing, go through the processes, read up on the guru notes, look for other niches.

 Really when I think about it, face book is not e-bay. People don't log into face book to buy stuff.

So unless you have something very special you are not likely to make enough to cover the costs of your time and overheads. And if you dress mutton up as lamb people will see through that too.

I needed something because age and physical work couldn't really continue for ever. The mind might be willing but the body isn't. Plus I have no where near enough money to retire on.

CHAPTER 3

Michael Dubhthaigh

Black Dog Dreaming

April came and so did a cyclone. For 2 days it hung around, one of the slowest moving cyclones in our history. 2 days of howling wind, no power, couldn't go outside. I sat inside and watched leaves, small branches and rain belt against the windows, watching palm trees bend, and their fronds shred, visibility limited to about 15 or 20 meters. Just a wall of rain coming at you.

After about 36 hours the wind died, and the rain fell even more heavily.

Absolutley hammering down, (some places received 170mm an hour. 8 Inches in the old language), the noise of rain on the tin roof was deafening. After about 4 hours it had stopped to a drizzle.

The road outside my house was flooded, people who were sick of being cooped up were starting to come out of their homes, People surveying the damage (in the dark). Debris scattered about everywhere, mostly vegetation, (luckily for us). I watched a woman walk her dog in knee deep water, (it was a big dog), cars stall in the flood water and guys pushing them out, other drivers hitting the water too fast and sailing into a street sign.

Crazy stuff, Peter Sellars would have been proud.

The down side was the looters were about too and there was a need to stay vigilant. Lots of people had evacuated and their homes were ripe for the picking.

It was another 5 days before I could get up to my bees, when I got there, there was not a lot to see. 5 hives on one property had been reduced to 2 struggling hives. I loaded them to take them home, try and get them back to production. The hives at the other property had disappeared. Washed away to who knew where. The property they were on was an absolute mess, trees down his garage in pieces lying against a tree that didn't fall in the wind.

I put the bees into new boxes, made a syrup for them and thought seriously about continuing with this hobby. I could always get back into it at some time in the future if I wanted. A month later I had sold them, along

Michael Dubhthaigh

Black Dog Dreaming

with most of my equipment.

 With the town getting back to normal, and the clean up making good progress I got stuck into the renovation and spent a few hours in the evening working through the FB program, sometimes for longer than I should have and only have a few hours sleep before going to work. My body clock was still coming alive in the wee hours after years of night work. Nothing like being fully alert at 2.00am.

For me looking back at the past is not the smartest thing to do. There is just too much crap involved. Once if I thought of something bad I would dismiss it and move on but it was becoming harder to do that.

The memories reside in some dark recess of my mind, and if they surface they stay with me for days, and I tell myself, that was dumb, you were an idiot, why didn't you do that. I have missed so many opportunities. So many stuff ups.

 I grew up in a rural area, I practically lived in a creek, catching yabbies, exploring around the sunken logs, looking at fish and eels, caught a small platypus one day, after a chase of a hundred meters or so, not counting the times we swam in circles.

I only caught him because he ran out puff before I did. I was just about out of it too. The deeper holes in the creek were about 15 feet and he would dive down and go like crazy to find a sunken log which made him a harder target to catch.

It was about a 100 meter walk back up the creek through a small set of rapids, and then across the creek and up the bank to home. Where I proudly showed my new found pet to the family. No one was really interested, so I took him back down to the creek and let him go.

And that is my favourite memory of my childhood. I was about 12 or 13. One day in my life that I always remember as a good day.

Michael Dubhthaigh

Black Dog Dreaming

There were other good times in that creek, like when it flooded we would go up to a railway bridge further upstream, jump in and let the current take us down stream to another bridge where would would climb out and go and do it all over again.

Often small animals and sometimes snakes would be also climbing up the bridge pylons to get out of the flooded creek, but they were climbing out for survival, not to go back and play in the flooded creek.

That creek is one memory that my mind brings up when I am down, I still the clear water, the sunken logs or old tree stumps, the platypus planning his next move me trying to second guess him. My lungs just about bursting trying to stay with him but determination keeping me under water until he made his next move then up for a quick breath and chase again.

Depression !. What a word!, it can mean a low spot in the terrain or how people feel about themselves. A loss of interest in work, hobbies and doing things they normally enjoy. A lack of ?, energy, difficulty sleeping or sleeping more than usual. Feeling irritable and hard to concentrate.

Depression is a hard slog. It will manage your life if you let it. The decisions you make. Your interactions with other people, etc.

A person may be depressed if, for more than two weeks, he or she has felt sad, down or miserable most of the time or has lost interest or pleasure in usual activities. I lost interest in things years ago. Driving a truck, sleeping and driving again, left little time for normal activity.

There is a list of other symptoms for depression, that include, behavior, feelings, physical, thoughts, then bi-polar, psychotic, post-natal, etc;

Everyone is different and there are any number of causes that can cause depression. Life events, and mental imbalances that lead to Bi-Polar behavior, and quite a few other behavioral imbalances.

Despair of a set of circumstances closing in on you. Post Natal depression.

Suicide happens regularly. A farmer for instance, his last cop failed, heavily in debt and the banks want their pound of flesh. No-where to go, aging, few options, to re-invent himself, so, down to the back paddock with a rifle, or take a long drive and over the edge of steep hill. It happens. A lot.

Michael Dubhthaigh

There is compilation of remedies and their ratings. Of 40 symptoms, only 6 of the remedies have a three thumbs up rating, all are medications combined with specialised therapy. All have side effects.

Melancholia is the main type of depression, and I suffer from it, sometimes very badly. (I don't do well on cloudy, rainy days either), It is a severe type and apart from medications not much else works.

Everything else seems to in a state of experiment or study.

My life has been a series of failures, Failure to finish studies I started, failure to resolve relationships, failure to finish projects, dreams that have slipped away, for any number of reasons, just bad decisions, bad actions. My worst decision was not taking the opportunity to (after about the 3rd time), to totally devote my self to my wife and kids. I was to screwed up with bitterness from the past.

Years later I learned tinnitus can lead to bad decisions. Maybe it was all that time in the creek. Working in noisy construction environments could not have helped either. Hindsight is 20/20 vision but what a way to recognise a bad decision, particulary one you cannot do anything about.

The buzzing noise in my head ruling my life, and essentially I have never been a happy, prosperous individual, although my health has generally been fairly robust. A few fleeting moments of serenity found when I was in the water, either swimming, in a boat, or just sitting on the bank with a fishing line.

Another hobby I had is making kayaks. Unfortunately, with the truck driving job all of my interests outside work went out the window. I just became a zombified shell of my former self. Another idea to finish my self off , was just paddle east, towards Sth America.

The answers I come up with as to why, or why not, I did or did not do something at a particular point in time usually involve pressure from someone, or some other pressure I created myself.

Debt is a pressure, but having money leads to bad decisions too and I had experience of both.

Michael Dubhthaigh

So what works for combating depression? Apart from medications   which all have side effects. No one seems to know. There is one remedy where they inject you with lithium. Lithium? Maybe I could insert a drip and run it from me to the ignition of my car and I won't have to worry about fuel?. Just get for another shot of lithium.

In Australia we have a group called Beyond Blue.

https://www.beyondblue.org.au/

It is one of a number of help organisations for sufferers of depression.

Out of 8 suicides every day in Australia, 6 are men and all are depression related.

365 x 6. = 2190. More than our national road toll.

Also in Australia around 800 people die each year from over doses of prescription medicine. Out of a population of 23 million.

What the statistics are in your country I do not know, but worldwide depression effects over 300 million people from the very poor to the very rich.
I would recommend having a look and looking at the organisations for helping people with depression. Have a look at their pages and do a few quiz's. It won't hurt. It might help you get a handle on what you are dealing with.

If you have a spare dollar or two, I am sure they would appreciate it. It might be used to help you.

CHAPTER 4

So, believing all the hype, and tuning my mind to positive (but a tiny voice in my gut saying noo you f'ing idiot), I put in a good amount of effort to make this face book drop shipping system happen.

Michael Dubhthaigh

Black Dog Dreaming

I wanted an income from something because I wasn't going to be able to continue in the old style of employment I was used to. Even with those jobs employers are saying your too old school, we need fresh faces.

I wanted to travel and spend time in other places, I have been to South America twice and have a desire to explore it further, America, New Zealand, Went on a Pacific cruise with my family back in the day. The urge to be out and about was alive and well.

There is just the small issue of money.

After running some FB ads for zero result I changed niches. So again, hours spent on a computer, populating it with products, editing photos, adjusting prices, adding new pages, checking the SEO. Adding a couple of tracking apps, and I am good to start running ads again, These look good, they have to be winners.

Nope. Just a dream, fast becoming a nightmare. The results varied only in the numbers reached, the website clicks, but still no one added anything to the cart. Ask for advice. ..."Don't drop ship clothes from China, the size variations will only get you people asking for refunds"...

Ok, ditch that niche and move onto niche plan F.

More hours in front of a computer, populating, editing photos, adjusting prices, deleting others, renaming pages, and off we go again. Good audience mix using the face book tool, good photo, catchy ad, put as a carosual ad, purchase. The definition of insanity was beginning to take hold.

Tinnitus and depression. A vanishing bank account, I am as mad as a cut snake.... Put me a straight jacket... Take me away..

Sitting on a step at my house looking at the beautiful day outside, but not able to do much because of my arm and other wounds, some which were still weeping blood. I was analyzing my-self. The first thought was

"....I am a f*****g idiot, pie in the sky dreamer."

Michael Dubhthaigh

E-Bay was easy, I never was full time or any thing but I had no problems.

With the artfire site it took a fair bit of time to populate it, but then it didn't need much maintenance. For sales I did maybe a few hours on a weekend swapping links, liking other peoples products and swapping
links, nothing to technical, keep abreast of postage and other price raises.

I listed the same items on Bonaza, no problems I made enough sales to keep me interested. The Amazon Affiliate site took some work to set up but I did learn coding, could add links etc, but after 12 months I gave it away. It was not really generating enough to keep me interested. Maybe If I had persisted?. Who knows?.

So, why was this FB idea not working? It was not new, I have seen different promotions on it before. Even face book have their own spin on how to use their platform and E-Bay use it to advertise as well.

CHAPTER 5

One way to live a reasonable life is to have a job, and do little else. You go to work, you pay your bills, put your kids through school and if you have enough you take a holiday once a year somewhere, maybe some fishing gear and a small boat for the weekends, a small workshop in the garage. You live

Black Dog Dreaming

frugally without trying to do anything entrepreneurial. My parents still live in the same house they bought 60 +years ago.

My father was a contract worker and he could make a years wages in 6 months, then it all became mechanised, so he turned to his carpentry skills, and made a living doing that for the next 25 or so years.

 In retirement he made things out of wood, vases, wooden fishing reels, tables etc, occasionally he sold some to friends but gave most away to relatives and family. I got a timber slab from him, sanded it and varnished it to a glass like finish and now use it as a coffee table.

My mother used to make clothes for friends and also sold some but gave much away. She used to display items at the local show where she won many ribbons.

After the show they would sell the items and some times she would make about $300. It was usually a timely boost to their pension. These days old age has caught up with them, arthritis and other ailments limit their activities.

In another life I was married a woman who had divorced and then partnered with me for about 20 years. We had twin daughters, who were an absolute joy to raise. One has her own travel agency and the other is a business consultant. Without a doubt they still help each other.

Both are married and are raising their own children. Paying off mortgages and all the things that come with modern living which requires both parents to work. Luckily, their husbands have trade skills.

So, making a coffee and back to sitting on the step wondering about all this, I wondered where did I go wrong, or more to the point what have I ever done that turned out right?.

I start something it doesn't work, I kick myself, beat my self up, so much unpaid effort, I invest money into it and get no bloody return.

Obviously I have nothing to offer anyone that would be worth paying for. The symptoms just get worse, more dark days, why does nothing f'ing work

Michael Dubhthaigh

for me. Am I the only one?

Nope ! .

Just like me the hosting shops blog is full of people having lots of visitors and no sales. People like me, who want to change the way they earn a living. The idea might be worthwhile but the track to achieve it is one of many. Face book is making a fortune of people who are dreaming.

The 60 day's refund deadline came and went, I missed it by a couple of days. Oh shit. I will keep trying but on a reduced scale, the future is looking bleak again, dark clouds on the horizon.

I am behaving like a schizophrenic. Calm on the outside, turmoil on the inside, and fooling no one. Some mornings I go to the shop over the road and get a coffee, the owner looks at me and asks "..What is wrong Michael, What is going on?".

The 1980's was a turbulent period. Australia had a new government which reinvented our economy.

The working class already struggling from the previous governments fiddling at the edges, now had to adjust to a new style of employment, as employers found it was easier to employ you as a contractor rather than have you on the books as an employee. For some it was ok, I survived during those times contracting but never really had the skills to leverage it into something substantial. I am not sure I really wanted to anyway.

The 1987 market crash bought disaster for many and I guess opportunities for others. For us living on a few acres just out of town in a converted shed, interest rates hit 19%. For a couple of years we battled on eventually subdividing a block and selling it. I priced it too low, but enough to cover the bank debt.

The guy who bought it immediately resold it for $6,000 more than he paid me.

Michael Dubhthaigh

Black Dog Dreaming

Banks wanting money, cost of living pressures, and just wanting to clear the debts and live without stress. Eventually we sold the rest of the property, on paper it looked good. I paid $17,500 when I bought it and the money for both blocks totaled over $100,000. After the debts were cleared we were left with about $14,000.

My wife and I parted company for awhile. I started a small business, hired the wrong people, I should have had more knowledge about the business than I had, plus I was drinking heavily.

Inevitability bankruptcy occurred and I was stuffed. Sometime in '93 I was back with my wife. We were still having the occasional spat, but I was working as a sole trader and she was running the money side of things and working as well.

Things were picking up, we bought a block of land and had a cottage built. I was subcontracting for a small company getting regular work and weekly pay checks. I added a couple of extensions to the house, the elder girls had left home, married and had children.

The twins were growing and enjoying life. Guitars and drums, Saturday mornings they would go to music classes. They were playing netball, and touch football. So everything was good, for awhile.

So maybe the simple life is best. If you have a job. Each week you bring home a wage (set by someone else), and after deductions you plan the outgoings for the forth coming week. Maybe even put some aside.

I think she had overcome her resentment of me, but for me I still had underlying problems. Plus my self esteem was not up there. I may have seemed happy and outgoing but always in the back of my mind were the ghosts of past failures. A lack of confidence. Even though it was years since I had been bankrupt the ghosts of the time still haunted me.

The question, Why? Why, why, indeed. As someone said, hindsight is 20/20 vision. and I did not want to commit to anything because there was still a

Michael Dubhthaigh

lot of volatility which raised its ugly head perodically and I would immediately feel resentment. But it could have been so much different. Unfortunately you cannot undo the past.

My parents were an issue too. They would come to visit but not stay long preferring to stay at my brothers place in the city. So this was the cause of more friction because my wife thought they preferred his children over mine.

More arguments. One time they came down and never visited us. Maybe my wife had a point.

My personal life would flow along smoothly for a while, and then, drama. It was as if no one wanted to see me content. If I was quietly minding my own business some one found a reason to stir the pot. She would go back to the past and then it was all downhill from there for a few days. Even weeks.

And so it like being on a roundabout of being knocked down, get up and try again, then stuff it, I am out of here.

After about 3 years in that house we divorced. She bought the papers home one day and asked me to sign them, I did and she took a deep sigh of regret. Me I wasn't happy either. It was time to start again, I left without a property settlement, and wondering what the future held.

Often now I look back and think what I should have or could have been, but there is still the memories of the screaming and yelling that my intuition tells me I would not have lasted anyway.

So it seems I have been traveling aimlessly for most of the past 20 years. Constant evolution and relocation, but still in the wrong place, doing the wrong things.

There are astrologers who do readings and they can suggest places you should live that would be more suitable for you. I might visit one, one day.

Where I live now is the birth place of my great grandmother on my

Michael Dubhthaigh

mothers side.

It is also where my grand father (on my fathers side), got married and there is a street named after my grand mothers brother who was killed in the first world war. If there are other relatives of mine here I do not know them.

Most probably moved with the ebb and flow of progress.

CHAPTER 6

Sometime in '95 I got sick. I rarely get sick but this was knock out, flat on your back sick, and it took about a week for me to recover. By the time I did I had lost my contract. Work was not hard to come by. A friend and I partnered together and we made good money.

He was a very fit man a few years younger than me, hardly drank, didn't smoke and a very good surfer. He was diagnosed with cancer. Eventually succumbing. He did it in style.

A day after some chemo treatment he went surfing, all his family were at the beach. He caught a couple of waves, and the last his wife and family saw of him, was him waving to them before he disappeared between the waves.

In '96 I started work for a large construction company and started on a project in a remote area. 28 days on and then 5 days off, 2 of them spent on an aeroplane, for the flights home and back. By March '98 I had had enough of that. The money was good, the work was hard but I was missing out on a lot at home.

Back home and back being a sole trader, I had even started playing the stock market. One morning I woke up to the news that the market had dropped, about 8.30 am the brokers secretary, called to ask what my position was (in case I had to put up margin), I was short and had about $8,000 in profit, my wife said you will lose that. By the end of the day I had. Bitch.

But inexperience, and revenge seeking were the real culprits. I could have just closed the trade there and then. That night we went to a party, I was not the most cheerful person there.

The twins were now in high school and I had the cottage at a point where it was finished. Then I came home one day and saw a real estate sign at the front of the house. My wife had decided to sell.

For all our troubles I am sure my wife loved me. She wanted to re-establish the relationship I declined.
I still haboured resentment from times past. It was an underlying revenge thing I guess, from back in the day of our struggles on that piece of acreage. That was a critical turning point for us. I just had no faith in my self. Too past baggage to contend with.

Our time at the new house was okay, We did a lot of renovations and landscaping, things were going well except for the arguments, and constant exchanges of sarcasm. During our last days together I had been setting up to pour a concrete driveway, and with the help of the boyfriend (now her

Black Dog Dreaming

husband), of one of the twins I poured the concrete after finishing work early one Friday.

The next morning I was up early and there was the boyfriends car parked on the freshly poured driveway. I lost it, in front of everyone. There are two ways to say things, but sometimes I have this build up of frustration and every it all comes out full of aggression.

So my wife, my daughters, and the step daughters all turned on me. That was it.

The true beginning of where I am now.

Every day I pass 4wd's cruising up the highway, fishing rods and often a boat on the roof rack and a mobile home hitched on the back, or a motor home towing a small 4wd. Grey nomads living the dream. I could have been one of them.

I realised years ago that whatever I was going to do was going to be hard. I never needed any help to make life harder. I knew that I was fully capable of making it damn near impossible to have a sense of inner peace, and feeling of satisfaction.

I look back and I see a nice cool path, green, mixed with the colours of lots of flowers, pinks and yellows and small clouds in the sky. A paradise, happy people along the path, waving, all happy to see the back of me.

 In front of me a hilly, dusty, road, with a scattering of stunted vegetation a hot sun shining through a heat haze.

Who knows where it leads to.

Michael Dubhthaigh

CHAPTER 7

I have never been a drug taker or user, I have over the years learnt that taking an aspirin won't kill you. For years I drank, sometimes heavily, I smoked, Getting pissed with my work mates, talking shit. Back in the day when a few beers at the local pub after a weeks work was pretty much a ritual.

In the early days it also led to a few fights, and a couple of run ins with the law eventually I grew up and tempered my behaviors. These days I rarely ever touch alcohol. The driving laws are pretty strict, and alcohol is quite expensive for the married working man. Most sales these days are for take

Black Dog Dreaming

home supplies. The local pubs are a dying breed.

After I was divorced, I formed a relationship with another woman. It lasted for about eight years. We still talk every now and then. But there was too much baggage in that relationship for it to ever be successful. She had 3 daughters. One of whom was an out and out drug addict, another daughter was constantly having relationship troubles.

We had moved from the town where our ex's lived and set up house about 80klms away. One day I came home from work and the drug addict daughter had moved in and taken over the lounge area, along with her two children.

That was the day I never had to wonder what it was like to jump out of the frying pan into the fire. I got to feel what it was like at that moment, and the burning went on for six months until she moved out.

She never went far, 100 meters down the road, set up a drug lab, and we were blessed with frequent drug induced visits.

Often destructive, so much so that her kids stayed at our place where they were cared for and sent to school.

One of the joys of having a job was not being home for most of the day, who knew what crazy stuff went on. Probably better I did not know.

Back then I still liked a beer on a warm day and in summer, to wind down after work I would relax on the patio with a cold beer and light up a smoke. Janis (my partner of the time), was a good masseuse, who knew acupuncture. She decided to experiment with a give up smoking treatment using acupuncture. So a couple of needles in my ear lobe (I forget if it was the left or right), and half and hour later I would be cured of this addiction.

Half and hour later and always the skeptic I went outside and lit up a smoke. I never noticed any changes it still tasted the same. I took a mouth full of beer. It tasted like crap.

Michael Dubhthaigh

I tried another beer and the same thing, tasted foul. Christmas day was a week later, I was offered a beer to join in the celebrations but left it sitting half empty on a table, the only other drinks I had that day was tea or soft drinks.   New Years day was no better.

I changed jobs later that year and spent the next four years traveling through out the state building electrical substations. Ten hour days, often six days a week, and in my managers role I would go in Sunday mornings and finalise the time sheets, subcontractors invoices and send everything to our head office.

Things were going not too badly, I was thinking of buying property, but the thought of a drug addict moving in and another bringing in her troubled relationships was not appealing. I was buying shares instead. My own kids were doing okay.

I went to one of my daughters weddings, when the other daughter got married and I was not invited because of what I did to their mother. I put it down to youth and her mothers constant put down of me probably caused her to take sides.

One thing about my new partner, (Janis), she had a way of explaining things to people. The relationship with my daughters improved immensely during my time with her and it is still in good standing today. For that I am grateful

It has been 7 years since Janis and I broke up. I had a brief liaison with another woman but it never really clicked. For the past 3 years I have lived on my own. Living a very monk like life, I drove a small truck, I slept, I drove a truck. No social life, the only people I had anything to do with were the people I picked things up from, and the people I delivered them too. That was it.

When I pulled the pin on that job, I was stuffed, completely and utterly dreading the phone ringing calling me in for another urgent delivery to some mine in that bouncing rough set of wheels.

Michael Dubhthaigh

Black Dog Dreaming

They say that to put some light on a subject or problem you should write it down. Maybe in these passages I will find a solution to my problem.
I have had various battles with depression over the years, an old friend gave me some advice along the lines of give your self a kick up the arse and get on with it.

This is common. But it doesn't always have the desired affect. A friend of mine was working on a remote liquid gas project making big bucks. He met a woman (the love of his life), set up house, he would be home about 1 week out of 4 and after 3 years of working and earning about $350,000.00 a year he departed with the credit card bill and the payments for a $60,000.00 4WD.

I have some idea how he felt. The "D" words come to mind, deceived, destroyed, devastated. I speak with him often, and we talk work, he is helping me find a job and giving me phone numbers of people to contact.

Anytime the subject is raised about that past relationship it still cuts him to talk about it. He doesn't say much and just puts the spin of its in the past and he has moved on. He says I saved him.

I did have something to do with his bust up from her. I went to their place during a Christmas break. I arrived with $1000.00 in my wallet. On my last night there, I left my wallet on the kitchen bench.

The next morning I was up early and thought I would go and fuel up my car before we had some breakfast. At the service station, I thought the wallet felt a bit light. Counted the money $300.00. Counted it again, $300.00. Paid for the fuel, $230.00 left. ?? Going through my head what I had spent the money on and nothing was adding up. There should have been at least $800.00 in my wallet.

Maybe I left $500.00 at home.? I would wait until I got back home before I said something. By the end of the week Mark was in the throes of leaving, trying to salvage what he could, which wasn't much. Not even his $20,000.00 boat which mysteriously disappeared, one night while he was at

Michael Dubhthaigh

another friends place. All her family including her parents were thieves.

For weeks he was lost. When I finally established contact with him he was in Sydney working on some small project.

Working does have its good points.

Unlike me, maybe he has put a couple of protections in place in case it happens again.

Maybe my problem is women. A boss once told me that.

CHAPTER 8

According to the Mayo Clinic, if you are on medication for depression allow time for trial and error. What works for one may not work for another. It is because ours brains have different circuitry.

Of the natural remedies St. Johns Wort figures prominently. But apparently it interacts with other drugs. Of all the medications for depression the side effects include, dry mouth, restlessness, drowsiness, vomiting, sexual problems, nausea, dizziness, constipation, low blood pressure, seizures and a few others.

So after a couple of months your depression has been bought under control, but you are now suffering from constipation. So you are on a course of laxatives, which may or may not interact with the depression medication, you are some where between a rock and a hard place.

It is estimated that there are 300 million people world wide who suffer from depression. The statistics say more woman than men suffer from depression. Men and young people are more likely to be suicidal. The majority of media chooses to focus on men and young people.

So how do you come up with 300million different prescriptions for the treatment of depression?. You can't
A lot of depression sufferers have disabilities, others are are in poverty, others particularly young people just see their position as hopeless.

Dealing with depression is difficult, the medical advice is to try "x" and see if it works if not we will try "y". This doesn't appeal to me, and living alone I have no one nagging me to go see someone. I have come close a few times to seeing a doctor, but then the sun came out, the feelings subsided and I regained a different perspective.

I applied for a job once and got it. About 3 months into the job I was told the bloke I replaced, left work one afternoon and was found the next morning hanging from a beam under his house. Apparently before he left

work on that afternoon, he was cheery, and cracking jokes.

His dark side was a broken marriage, child support for kids he couldn't visit, and who knows what other issues were giving him a feeling of despair and hopelessness.

The politicians will say he was avoiding his responsibilities, he was selfish, he was irresponsible. Without wanting to go to much into politics, I will say their intervention into personal lives always leads to disaster. The major beneficiaries being the legal profession.

Thirty years or so after politicians introduced these laws, they are now dealing with a large and getting larger homeless population comprised of adults, and young people, Young people who have never had a father figure, drugs and high suicide rates in men and young people and add, families breaking apart because of government policies relating to cost of

Michael Dubhthaigh

living, electricity, which loaded onto other household commitments, child care, etc, and other costs lumped onto families by the lower tiers of government (state and local), car registrations, land taxes etc.

Before our kids went to school and sometimes after school we would drop them at this lady's place who used to baby sit about 7 or 8 kids from different families. She lived in an old style hi-set wooden house, she had a large yard, with swings and a sand pit. Then in the early nineties the government thought it should control child care.

They made it illegal for woman like the one we left our kids with to do child care with out some sort of certificate and basically having to do a whole building renovation to become compliant, or demolish and start again.

 Now the whole system is a dogs breakfast. People getting in and trying to make money setting up child care business's and nearly all relying on a government subsidies to stay afloat, some crashing and burning completely. Parents relying on tax breaks to afford the costs.

And they wonder why more and more people suffer from depression and the use of prescription drugs has seen health costs blow through the roof.

Yet they still persist in making "adjustments" to their "program" to fix a mess entirely of their own making.

There is a site called Moodgym, which has been put up by the Australian National University.

It is designed to help people with depression. For more serious cases like me, it recommends seeing a health professional. Something I fight about with myself all the time.

Today I am good, tomorrow I might do something or something could happen that will send me into a dark hole. So that is my reason for not seeing any one. I don't want to a permanent fixture on some ones couch, or popping down a series of pills every morning for the rest of my life.

Michael Dubhthaigh

One person I know starts his day with 10 different pills, all set out by his wife so he doesn't mix them up. Probably without her he would not take any.

I try and keep some sort of grip on reality. A wish to die and end it all is balanced by " I haven't finished making xxxxx" or " who will clean up my things" or I don't have enough to leave the kids anything" "I can do better, make an (another) effort", I don't want to go as a total failure. Etc.

The counter thoughts are, "you have tried so many things and they all turn to crap", "you are practicing the definition of insanity by keeping trying. Give it up", " My grandfather died in his mid 60's, I am not that much younger so don't worry about the difference". " you are stuffed, in debt from the last venture".

And so a mental conflict rages, but only when there is some sunshine appearing in my life. In the dark hole state, there are very few thoughts that I can remember. Even a day later when I emerge from the dark hole, I only remember a grey, unwelcoming, place that overwhelms me. And there I live sometimes for days at a time. I don't want to be there, but I submit and eventually I force myself to do something and I improve.

Mood gym perfectly describes depression as a dissociation or a disconnect from ourselves.

Defeating the black dog is never easy. It might be dormant for 10 years and it all comes back in a big rush. The black dog awakens and depending on the size of the failure or set back suffered, or in the case of ambulance and police officers, fireman etc; the constant memories of tragedies, the outcome could be very bad.

Two main reasons people suffer unhappy feelings are things they have screwed up themselves or something someone else has done or said, or for the more serious cases, a series of setbacks spanning many years and a view that the future will be no different. The reason we feel like we do is our fault. We demand too much of our selves or let others demand too much of us.

With my ex nothing I did was never good enough, quick enough, or some other criticism. Constant parroting eventually feeds into the esteem part of your self and you believe it.

I knew a guy who was working away from home and most nights he would go to a club for a few drinks and flirt with the barmaids. His girlfriend had come down to visit him one weekend and he took her to a club for dinner.

A requirement for entry to the club was you had to fill out a small form for temporary membership. As they were filling out the form he turned to his girlfriend and asked... " Can you pretend your my sister I'm trying to hook up with one of the barmaids".

When asked about her reaction he just said she went home the next morning. That she was someone with whom he never desired to have a relationship with. How she felt I can only imagine.

 Self esteem is a big issue when dealing with depression. In personal relationships there is a need to feel wanted. When the relationship is new the break up is easy, if it is mature and you have jointly held things for years then it is easy to add to the pain by self destructing. Keeping yourself together is no easy task.

CHAPTER 9

I have never been to a doctor for depression. When I have had to go to a doctor for some ailment only 2 have picked that I have depression. How they did I do not know, because both times I was visiting about a physical problem and feeling reasonably robust.

Maybe it is the hound dog look or something?, but I gave an honest answer both times.

We are faced with choices. Like the woman earlier who suffered rejection, she would have two choices, of which road to go down. She could blame herself for feeling bad or put it down to incompatibility. Whatever, she would still need to rebuild her self esteem.

 It would be a memory that would not go away in a hurry, and even trying to change your thinking would be difficult. Your thoughts will always be competing against the thoughts of rejection. How long would it take? 6 mths, 12 mths, or until she found a new partner who had respect for her.

My former partner Janis had many self help books. Apparently her marriage was violent and chaotic. Mentally at that time I was okay, there was the odd dark moment, but only minor compared to what is happening now.

I had outside interests to keep me occupied, I was employed, my biggest dramas were at home with the craziness of what Janis had to deal with. Two young kids with a drug screwed mother who it seemed no amount of help would cure or even temper her bad behavior.

Being a mother Janis persisted trying to help, each time the result was the same a the previous time, if we moved, within a short time I would come home to a pile of clothes and bedding in my lounge. History repeating, essentially it was the reason we broke up. If we were too far away, then Janis would have to fly home because her daughter was in trouble again.

It was a revolving door I didn't want to keep passing through. It was frustrating to watch and, thoroughly draining mentally, not to mention expensive, any comments I made had no effect.

Talking to Janis recently and she told me she realised she had to stop running after her daughter every time she called. She now lives at an address unknown to her daughter. Despite all that has happened to her she still has good (outwardly at least), self esteem. Maybe there is something in those self help books.

On my good days I tell myself there is some one worse off than me, and to be thankful that I am still walking on the top side.

It is the youth I find hard to comprehend. Last year for instance a young footballer committed suicide in the town I live in. He had the world at his feet, playing in the top grade and not too far away from getting a gig in the national league. Or a friends 21 year old son, single, working, living at home, no drugs involved, but for some reason decided to go to the other side.

What are we doing?.

Michael Dubhthaigh

Black Dog Dreaming

In a nut shell I know my problem. I am aging and am trying to find a different way of making a dollar, struggling to renew myself and I understand that change can bring pain, as you get older it is more difficult, the energy is not there, you relapse into previous disasters, and it is difficult to keep going, demanding that things fall into place. A last spin of the wheel?.

Losers give up and winners keep going?. Maybe winners know early enough when something will not work, cut their losses and search for a better idea, taking the lessons from the last mistake. What is the point of banging your head against a wall.

 Young people ? Is technology creating just a lot of lonely people? Has it created such a sense of unreality that it overwhelms them? Who am I to talk, he who paid $3500 for a dream.

The old style jobs I worked in are still there, the younger generation will always win over me in any application because they have a longer lifespan, plus these days employers look for papers with fancy writing
over experience.

As I said earlier. I am to "Old School". Health and Safety doesn't like me.

I never finished my studies and have no intention of completing them. There is no point, any employment gained by doing that would only be short term. Construction in this country is heavily regulated.

I need to try something new. Writing is not new to me, Back in the day I have written for 4wd magazines on a part time basis, somewhere along the way I stopped doing it. Maybe now I have come full circle.

The road behind me still looks like paradise, the one in front looks very uninviting..I feel tired, should I keep going?. I look behind and everyone is happy.

Michael Dubhthaigh

CHAPTER 10

Writing this I have had different emotions at different stages, and sometimes it is hard to stay coherent because I have many other thoughts running through my mind. Someone said play music while you write.

Someone else said listening to happy music will lift your mood. When I am down I have no desires to listen to anything or talk to anyone, or read anything.

Eventually I force myself to do something, then I will move onto something else, so long as it is easy and I cannot stuff it up, one small achievement leads to something more difficult until I am back at my normal capabilities.

Inspirational stories are good medicine.

In 1997 there was a landslide at a ski resort in the Snowy region of Australia. 3 days later rescuers found one survivor (Stuart Diver), 18 others including his wife perished. These day's he is on the speakers circuit, and manages a snow sports school at the same resort that bore the brunt of the avalanche.

He says to lean on professionals for psychological help. The day he was rescued he was dealing with the euphoria of being alive and the despair of his wifes passing. For years he had to deal with the those conflicting thoughts and the loneliness of losing his wife and 17 friends. He also contemplated suicide.

He remarried only to have his second wife die of cancer, and he now brings up their daughter.

He wrote a book called "Survivor"

Many of us who suffer depression are not superstars and will probably never be superstars. Our lives are bound by struggling with the norms

and not so normal things in society. Repetitive destructive events and other circumstances dwell in our minds to tell us get out, leave now.

We constantly battle conflicts in our minds making it hard to concentrate. On those days motivation is near impossible.

Getting out of that situation is hard and for those who have not experienced it, it is hard to comprehend.

A bloke I once knew was a hard worker, and hard drinker. Years later I was working with someone who shared a unit with him and he was off the grog and living a clean life. Saving money and had a new motorbike. After finishing work one Friday he got on his motorbike and went home for the weekend. He was found hanging from a tree in his mothers yard on Sunday morning.

What went wrong?. The average person will never know.

It is the black dog, he never goes away he might sleep for a while but he always comes back and bites, usually when things are looking good. It is a life long battle of connection and disconnect.

There are numerous sites for depression The Australian sites all link to each

Michael Dubhthaigh

other. Moodgym, headspace, beyond blue, reach out .com etc.

Overseas readers of this can goggle depression / anxiety to get the responses for your country. Although I have never seen a psychologist or doctor specifically for depression I have found these web sites useful. For adults as well as youths. If you don't want help try self help, there is plenty out there.

About the Author.

 Michael Dubhthaigh is an Australian based writer who writes using the Gaelic translation of his English surname. He tries to live in harmony with himself, writing, creating things from wood, fixing up houses and putting weired things for sale on E-Bay. A lot of his friends still work in construction, and often he wishes he was with them working on the latest signature project.

Quite a few people he has worked with have passed on, some close friends, others just casual acquaintances, not all from natural causes. As he says at "his age he will attend more funerals than marriages".

Married to a hermoso Colombiano mujer. Long haul flights is not one of his favourite ways to travel.

He has a blog about bees. https://www.lowflyingbee.com/

Michael Dubhthaigh

Black Dog Dreaming

Michael Dubhthaigh